**For Ben and my two little bugs,
Emily and Annabelle
- C. E.**

**For my mom,
who is anything but conventional
- Y. I.**

LCCN 2019900121
ISBN 9781943147663

Text copyright © 2019 by Christine Evans
Illustrations copyright © 2019 Yasmin Imamura

Published by The Innovation Press
1001 4th Avenue, Suite 3200, Seattle, WA 98154

www.theinnovationpress.com

Printed and Bound by Shenzhen Reliance Printing Co. Ltd.
Production Date: October 2023
Plant location: Nanling Longgang, Shenzhen

Cover lettering by Nicole LaRue
Cover art by Yasmin Imamura
Book layout by Rose Clemens

EVELYN THE ADVENTUROUS ENTOMOLOGIST

THE TRUE STORY OF A
World-Traveling Bug Hunter

by
CHRISTINE EVANS

illustrated by
YASMIN IMAMURA

Back in 1881 when Evelyn Cheesman was born, most people thought girls should be quiet, clean, and covered with lace. And little Victorian girls definitely weren't supposed to go on bug hunts.

But Evelyn went anyway.

She explored forests and splashed
in ponds with her brothers and sister.

She crawled in mud and stuffed
her pockets with bugs.

Jars of glowworms sparkled while she dreamed
about the world beyond her small English home.

Many years later, Evelyn applied to veterinary college. She longed to help sick animals.

However, it was the early 1900s. Women couldn't vote. They rarely went to college. And they certainly weren't allowed to be vets.

So, she did the next best thing and trained as a canine nurse, hoping the veterinary college would open to women after a few years. Evelyn cared for sick greyhounds, bulldogs, and terriers.

She fed the dogs, took their temperatures, and gave them medicine. But in her heart she still wanted to be a vet.

One day, Evelyn's friend Grace wrote that her cousin, Professor Lefroy, was desperate for someone to run London Zoo's insect house. A woman had never been in charge of the insect house before.

But Evelyn went anyway.

A single beetle paddled in a giant tank, but the rest of the insect house echoed. It had been neglected while zookeepers, along with millions of other men, served in the First World War.

Evelyn agreed to give the job a try.

She scooped insects from
London's ponds and streams.

She asked local children to find caterpillars, beetles, and snails to star in her exhibits.

She studied entomology, exploring insect books for wonders to share.

After a few weeks of bug hunting, the tanks were full.
And so was Evelyn's heart. In the insect house, Evelyn
spun stories for curious visitors. She showed them tiny
ants carrying pine needles to build their homes, a water
snail crawling up glass with its muscular foot, and
butterflies sipping nectar. Crowds swarmed the insect
house to watch Evelyn's bugs creep and slide and scurry.

Evelyn still dreamed about places beyond her small world, but now she also dreamed about insects never studied, and about stories untold. Even when the veterinary college opened its doors to women at last, Evelyn knew she never wanted to leave the world of insects.

In 1924 she heard about an expedition to study tropical insects. In those days, women scientists and explorers were rare. People thought it wasn't safe. Women should be at home.

But Evelyn went anyway.

After traveling on a rolling ocean for over 5,000 miles,
Evelyn explored the Pacific islands from sunrise to sunset.

She chased centipedes, caught butterflies, and stalked giant land snails.

On the island of Gorgona, Evelyn stumbled into a sticky curtain of spiderwebs. As the spiders watched, she bit and pulled and kicked the threads, but there was no escape!

Then Evelyn remembered the metal nail file in her pocket. She hacked each sticky strand one by one and emerged from her cocoon.

On the island of Nuku Hiva, Evelyn wanted to scale a steep cliff that she was sure would reveal some interesting insects. The villagers told Evelyn that only one man had ever climbed it. They told her not to go.

But Evelyn went anyway.

After hours of climbing, Evelyn was rewarded with buzzing bees and wasps, beetles, and grasshoppers. However, she soon realized she'd made a terrible mistake. She'd forgotten the fresh limes she planned to squeeze and drink.

As Evelyn hunted for a stream, she slipped.
She grasped at plants as she kept tumbling . . .

Until she clung to a bush and stopped. All alone, Evelyn had to save herself. She inched slowly up the cliff like a caterpillar.

Evelyn had survived another adventure. And her backpack full of insects had survived, too.

Evelyn kept traveling and studying insects. In 1925 she sailed to Tahiti where she discovered a new species of grasshopper.

In 1934 she explored New Guinea and found a new species of beetle.

In 1938 she found a new blue orchid on
top of an extinct volcano in Waigeo.

And in 1955, the Queen of England awarded Evelyn an OBE—Officer of the Most Excellent Order of the British Empire—for her services to science.

Evelyn never stopped working—even after her hair turned white and her body ached. For nearly thirty years, this adventurous entomologist climbed mountains, explored jungles, and collected insects.

Then she spun her stories into books inspiring others to be like Evelyn . . .

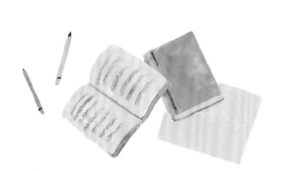

And go anyway.

INTERVIEW WITH DR. ALEXANDRA HARMON-THREATT

What is your favorite insect? Why do you love them?

I primarily study bees. There are so many reasons to love them, including the important role they play in ensuring we live in a colorful and delicious world by pollinating flowers. Bees also come in a wide variety of colors and sizes, which makes them interesting to study.

What is your favorite insect fact?

This is a difficult question, but probably my favorite fact is that insects are the most diverse group on the planet. We often overlook them but they are everywhere.

What are you studying at the moment?

My lab is really interested in understanding how disturbances like fire and pesticides affect pollinator diversity and conservation. We hope to improve conservation efforts by learning about habitats that can support large numbers of insects and figuring out what is special about them.

All photos courtesy of Dr. Harmon-Threatt

How did you get to be an entomologist?

I didn't know entomology existed until I went to college, and I certainly didn't know you could make a living studying insects. But I was lucky enough to find a program that let me study plant pollination during my sophomore year. I fell in love with research and decided I wanted to switch to insects because I found them more interesting.

Did you love insects when you were a kid?

I grew up in Chicago so there weren't a lot of natural areas to explore daily, except our yard. I loved being outside but there weren't a lot of insects around. However, I distinctly remember working in the garden with my mom and she was telling me how bees pollinated the flowers. I was about five years old and when I looked around our garden, I saw many flowers but few bees. I became super worried about making sure our flowers were pollinated so I started moving pollen from flower to flower. Lilies, tulips, and roses were cross-pollinated that day by my tiny fingers. I remember being concerned about bees even then.

Have you ever been stung by an insect?

I am stung constantly by sweat bees, which like to lap sweat off your skin. While we are working they will crawl all over our hands, up our sleeves, and under our shirts. They sting us when they are startled and are trying to escape. I've also been stung by caterpillars with urticating hairs (that cause itching and irritation).

Have you ever discovered a new insect?

Some of our work takes us to remote areas of the country, and in these areas, the insects are not well studied. In these places, we have found a number of new and rare insects. We then work with an insect taxonomist who verifies that they are in fact new, undescribed species and will eventually give these new species names. It can take a very long time to determine if a species is new and requires a lot of comparison to other similar insects.

Have you ever found yourself in a sticky situation while studying insects?

I often see lots of venomous snakes when I'm out trying to catch insects. While looking around and paying attention to the bees and butterflies on flowers, you always have to remain aware of your feet because quite often you will almost step on a rattlesnake. I've also seen evidence of mountain lions in areas we were working in, and that makes it a bit hard to focus on the insects. Once we were studying the effects of grazing, and the cows became very curious about us, and they all ran over and surrounded us and our car. Cows can be quite dangerous, so the team was a bit nervous, but with some loud noises they moved away.

ABOUT LUCY EVELYN CHEESMAN

Lucy Evelyn Cheesman, known by her middle name, was born in 1881. She was often ill as a child and spent a lot of time in bed. But the sickly child turned into a strong woman who persisted despite danger, disease, and disapproval.

She started her working life as a governess in England, and then trained as a canine nurse, taking care of sick dogs. But it was her career in entomology (the study of insects) that led her on a path virtually uncharted for women at that time. She became the first woman curator of the London Zoo's insect house and turned it from a dusty, abandoned room into a thriving attraction at the zoo.

Evelyn's first overseas expedition was in 1924 with a group of other scientists. But she soon grew frustrated and wanted to set out alone, to be in charge of her own travel, and to follow her passion. In 1925, her solo adventure began. It was not without peril. Evelyn spent one night wet, shivering, and completely lost on Tahiti while exploring and collecting insects. She eventually found her way back to camp, exhausted and her clothes in ruins. But in true Evelyn style, her rucksack of specimens survived.

Evelyn did not see herself as courageous for embarking on eight solo expeditions. She wrote in her autobiography, "It is not so much courage that is called for, but endurance." Evelyn endured difficult conditions, and survived dangerous situations, to collect over seventy thousand specimens—some that hadn't been recorded by scientists before—so they could be studied at London's Natural History Museum.

Her last expedition was in 1954, at the age of seventy-three, after hip surgery. In 1955 Queen Elizabeth II awarded Evelyn with an OBE—Officer of the Most Excellent Order of the British Empire—for her services to science.

As well as studying insects and their origins, Evelyn was a prolific weaver of stories for adults and children. Her first books, *Everyday Doings of Insects* and *The Great Little Insect*, were published in 1924. She went on to publish a total of sixteen books, including two autobiographies.

Even after she retired from exploring, Evelyn worked at the Natural History Museum in London. She died in 1969 at the age of eighty-eight. But her collections and stories live on, and scientists are still making new discoveries thanks to Evelyn. So far, at least sixty-nine species have been named after her.

Bibliography

Cheesman, Evelyn. *Things Worth While*. London: Readers Union, 1958.

Cheesman, Evelyn. *Time Well Spent*. London: Hutchinson, 1960.

Laracy, Hugh. *Watriama and Co.* Acton, Australia: ANU Press, 2013. http://dx.doi.org/10.22459/WC.10.2013.

Lotzof, Kerry. "Lucy Evelyn Cheesman: The Woman Who Walked." Natural History Museum, March 8, 2018. www.nhm.ac.uk/discover/lucy-evelyn-cheesman.html.

Natural History Heroes, "Evelyn Cheesman," produced by Ellie Sans, aired September 8, 2016, on BBC Radio 4. www.bbc.co.uk/programmes/b06flmd3.

Natural History Museum. "Evelyn Cheesman." YouTube video, 2:54. Posted February 14, 2011. www.nhm.ac.uk/nature-online/science-of-natural-history/biographies/evelyn-cheesman/index. html.